Daly's Bartenders' Encyclopedia

A Pre-Prohibition Cocktail Book

Tim Daly

Historic Cookbooks of the World
Kalevala Books, Chicago

"Drink the first. Sip the second slowly. Skip the third."
— Knute Rockne, 1888–1931

Daly's Bartenders' Encyclopedia:
A Pre-Prohibition Cocktail Book

Joanne Asala, Editor
Historic Cookbooks of the World

Rowan Grier, Series Editor
Classic Cocktail Guides
and Retro Bartender Books

Classic Cocktail Guides and Retro Bartender Books and *Historic Cookbooks of the World* are published by Kalevala Books, an imprint of Compass Rose Technologies, Inc., PO Box 409095, Chicago, IL 60640. Titles published by Kalevala Books are available at special quantity discounts to use as premiums and sales promotions or for academic use. For more information, please write to the Director of Special Sales, Compass Rose Technologies, Inc., PO Box 409095, Chicago, IL 60640 or contact us through our Web site, www.CompassRose.com.

Editors' Note

Some ingredients found in vintage cocktail guides are unavailable or hard to come by today. Check out our resource guide at the back for vendors who specialize in hard-to-find ingredients and websites with information on how to recreate classic cocktails and cocktail ingredients.

ISBN: 978-1-880954-32-4

Daly's Bartenders' Encyclopedia

Tim Daly

Classic Cocktail Guides and Retro Bartender Books

DALY'S

Bartenders' Encyclopedia.

A COMPLETE CATALOGUE

**Of the Latest and Most Popular Drinks, with
a number of original ones by the Author,
and the proper method of
serving them.**

TIM DALY, Publisher.

WORCESTER, MASS.
1903.

PRICE, 50 CENTS.

Classic Cocktail Guides and Retro Bartender Books

INTRODUCTORY.

N presenting this work to the public I take great pride in stating that it is the result of close observation and study of the proper method of preparing and serving drinks, as well as my personal experience of twenty years behind the bar in some of the most exclusive cafes in Massachusetts, Rhode Island, New York, Maryland, New Jersey, Illinois, Minnesota, and Washington, D. C., and embodies all the well-known and popular drinks known to the trade, and a number of new and original ones, by the author, heretofore unpublished, but served by him in such well-known hostelries as the Parker House in Boston, famous the world

3

over for the deliciousness of its cocktails, punches, and other mixed drinks, and for the excellence of the service.

In reference to my personal experience will say I began my career as bell boy in the Lincoln House in Worcester, Mass., in 1882, and from the start devoted strict attention to the bar business, which soon resulted in procuring me the position of bartender, which vocation I have since followed, and have exerted every energy to have the art of mixing drinks brought to the stage of perfection. I now take pleasure in presenting the result of my experience, study and research to the public in a concise manner, enabling them to prepare a palatable concoction, and serving it in an appetizing form.

In order to produce the most satisfactory results the best ingredients should be used in every instance, and if this is done, you will have a delicious concoction from every formula herein contained. I do not wish to pose as the only exponent of the art of mixology, but desire to impress the importance

4

of the following apparently insignificant details, which should be closely followed:

Always have glass and silverware dry and polished.

See that trays are clean and dry.

When dry cocktails are ordered, never use a cherry or olive unless customer especially requests it.

In squeezing lemons for bar use, strain through fine sieve or cheese-cloth, so that concoction will not appear cloudy.

In mixtures where ice is used in serving-glass, care should be exercised to have it clean and clear.

Do not fill serving-glass so it will overflow.

Where draught beer and ales are used the pipes should be frequently and thoroughly cleaned, and faucets kept polished.

In drinks where limes or lemons are used, extreme caution should be exercised to avoid having seeds in serving-glass.

In preparing hot drinks of any description, the serving-glass should be thoroughly

5

rinsed in hot water, and a spoon placed in glass, so as to minimize the risk of breakage and enable you to serve the drink thoroughly hot.

Bottled liquors of all descriptions should be kept lying down so as to keep the corks moist and avoid evaporation.

Have your glass and bar towels clean.

Bitters and cordials of every description should be kept in the original bottles, with the labels clean and attractive, and should never, under any circumstance, be refilled.

When patrons request cigars instead of drinks, always serve them in a glass if silver tray is not available.

In conclusion, will add it is hardly necessary to enumerate the various little details which every bartender should be familiar with, but will merely suggest keep everything connected with your bar and back bar thoroughly clean and attractive, and you will procure the patronage of the most desirable class of customers, and be enabled to serve them with mutual satisfaction.

Very truly yours,
TIM DALY.

Historic Cookbooks of the World

UNIONISM THE FUNDAMENTAL
PRINCIPLE OF EFFICIENCY.

AM a firm believer in unions, as they tend to improve the condition of their members financially as well as socially, and insure to proprietors employing members thereof competent and reputable men.

My personal connection with the Bartenders' Union for a number of years has convinced me of the utility of organizations of that nature, and since 1889, when I proposed forming a local union in Worcester, Mass., and in which the outlook was very auspicious until after the election, which resulted in no license, I have been a strong adherent to the cause. Our Union has been the means of elevating the bartender to the same social standing as men in other professions whom necessity requires to earn their living. Not

8

only this, but the Union has brought about a feeling of affiliation among our members which naturally benefits their employers, from the fact that bartenders no longer harbor feelings of jealousy or antipathy toward each other, which, in the past, resulted in their making disparaging and detrimental remarks concerning competitors' stock, eac.

Fraternally yours,

TIM DALY.

INDEX.

10

Historic Cookbooks of the World

12

Classic Cocktail Guides and Retro Bartender Books

13

14

15

CHAMPAGNE FLIP.

Use medium size thin bar glass.

1 fresh, cold egg.
1 bar spoonful of sugar.
4 or 5 very small lumps of ice.
Fill glass with champagne, shake well and quickly, taking care to have shaker fit tightly over the glass.

This drink should be consumed as expeditiously after being served as possible.

For the high liver with that tired feeling in the early hours of the morning, the above is the acme of perfection.

BISHOP.

Use a large bar glass.

1 spoonful of sugar dissolved in half a wine-glass of water.
1 or 2 dashes of lime juice.
2 or 3 dashes of orange bitters.
½ glass of fine ice.
3 dashes of Jamaica rum.
Fill the glass with claret, spoon well, dress the top with fruit, and serve with straws.

17

GIN DAISY.

Use a mixing glass.

1 spoonful of sugar.
3 or 4 dashes of lime juice.
Half fill the glass with fine ice.
1 squirt of seltzer water.
Dissolve with the lime juice.
1 wine-glass of Holland gin.
$\frac{1}{2}$ pony glass of white curacoa.
Spoon well, then take a fancy stem glass,
put in fruit in season, strain the mixture into
glass, and serve.

JAMAICA RUM FIX.

Use a large bar glass.

$\frac{1}{2}$ spoonful of sugar dissolved in a little
water.
2 or 3 dashes of lime juice.
$\frac{1}{2}$ pony glass of pineapple syrup.
1 wine glass of Jamaica rum.
Fill the glass with fine ice, spoon well, decorate the top with fruit, and serve with
straws.

BRANDY DAISY.

Use a large bar glass.

$\frac{1}{2}$ spoonful of sugar.

2 or 3 dashes of lime juice; dissolve in a little water.

1 pony glass of yellow chartreuse; fill the glass with fine ice.

1 glass of brandy (Hennessey).

Mix well with spoon; place the fruit in a fancy stem glass, strain the ingredients into it, and serve.

SHERRY AND EGG.

Use a fancy stem glass.

Pour a small quantity of wine into the glass to prevent the egg from sticking to the glass; then break a fresh egg into the glass, place the glass on the bar, and fill it with sherry wine, and serve.

For a person who is run down, or threatened with nervous debility, there is no decoction so far discovered which can equal it as a stimulant, it being one of the instances when it is quality not quantity that counts.

19

JAMAICA RUM AND DAISY.

Use a mixing glass.

2 or 3 dashes of gum syrup.

2 or 3 dashes of orange curacoa.

2 or 3 dashes of lime juice.

1 wine glass of Jamaica rum.

Half fill the glass with fine ice. Mix well with spoon, strain into a cocktail glass, and serve.

EGG LEMONADE.

Use a large bar glass.

1 spoonful of sugar.

5 or 6 dashes of lemon juice.

1 fresh egg.

Fill the glass with fine ice, and the balance with water.

Shake well with a shaker, strain into a large thin glass, and serve.

A very refreshing beverage, containing considerable nutrition, and entirely without a vestige of alcohol.

SODA LEMONADE.

Use a large bar glass.

1 spoonful of sugar dissolved in a squirt of seltzer.

2 or 3 dashes of lemon juice.

1 bottle of plain soda water.

Fill the glass with fine ice, spoon well, and serve with straws.

BEEF TEA.

Use a small china mug.

$\frac{1}{2}$ teaspoonful of the beef extract.

Fill the mug with hot water, put in little salt and pepper to suit taste, and serve with a spoon.

On a cold, blustry day the above is unsurpassed for warming the system and imparting strength and vigor to the entire body without the aid of any alcoholic ingredients.

LEMONADE.

Use a large bar glass.

2 spoonfuls of sugar.

5 or 6 dashes of lemon juice.

Fill the glass with fine ice, the balance with water; shake well, decorate with fruit. and serve with straws.

Historic Cookbooks of the World

ALE SANGAREE.

Use a mixing glass.

1 spoonful of sugar.
Dissolve in half a wine glass of water.
Fill the glass with ale, grate a little nutmeg on top, and serve.

BRANDY FIX.

Use a mixing glass.

½ spoonful of sugar dissolved in a little seltzer water.
2 or 3 dashes of lemon juice.
½ pony glass of pineapple syrup.
1 or 2 dashes of chartreuse (yellow).
1 wine glass of brandy (Hennessey).
Fill the glass with shaved ice, spoon well, decorate with fruit, and serve with straws.

SODA NEGUS.

(About one quart.)

1 pint port wine.
12 lumps loaf sugar.
8 cloves.

22

Bar spoonful of grated nutmeg.

Place ingredients in a saucepan; warm and stir well, but do not allow to boil.

Pour into bowl, and add bottle of soda.

The above makes a most delightful, mild, hot drink for a home party, and can be indulged in by moderate drinkers without any unpleasant consequences.

ST. CROIX RUM FIX.

Use a mixing glass.

½ spoonful of sugar dissolved in a little water.

2 or 3 dashes of lime juice.

½ pony glass of pineapple syrup.

1½ wine glass of St. Croix rum.

Fill the glass with fine ice, spoon well, decorate the top with fruit, and serve with straws.

OLD-FASHIONED GIN COCKTAIL.

Use a gin glass.

1-3 of a glass of water.

½ spoonful of sugar; dissolve the sugar well.

23

2 or 3 dashes of bitters (Angostura).

1 small lump of ice.

2-3 glass of gin.

Twist a piece of lemon peel and drop in the glass. Mix well with a spoon, and serve.

This drink is extremely popular with elderly persons who have been good fellows for a generation.

RHINE WINE COBBLER.

Use a mixing glass.

1 spoonful of sugar.

1 wine glass of seltzer water; dissolve well with a spoon.

1½ wine glass of Rhine wine.

Fill the glass with fine ice, spoon well, decorate with orange, pineapple, berries, etc., and serve with straws.

Commended highly by the royalty of Germany, and called for extensively by the upper class of the fatherland.

GIN FIX.

Use a mixing glass.

½ teaspoonful of sugar dissolved in a little seltzer.

2 or 3 dashes of lime juice.

24

½ pony glass of pineapple syrup.
1 wine glass of honeysuckle gin.
Fill the glass with fine ice, spoon well, dress with fruit, and serve with straws.

'ALF AND 'ALF.

Use large ale glass.

½ glass of porter; fill the balance of the glass with old ale; see that the drink is cold.

An old English favorite in vogue for many generations, with prospects of many more.

GIN AND TANSY.

Use a whiskey glass.

This is an old-fashioned but excellent tonic, and is prepared by steeping a bunch of tansy in a bottle of Holland gin, which extracts the essence.

In serving, place the glass, with a lump of ice dropped into it, before the customer, and let him help himself from the bottle containing the preparation.

25

WHISKEY JULEP.

Use a mixing glass.

1 spoonful of sugar.

½ wine glass of seltzer water.

Take 4 or 5 sprigs of mint, and press them in the seltzer water until the flavor of the mint is extracted; fill the glass with fine ice.

1 wine glass of whiskey; shake well, decorate with mint, orange, pineapple, berries, etc.

Dash with Jamaica rum, sprinkle a little sugar on top, and serve with straws.

A most palatable decoction, which leaves an extremely pleasant aroma to the breath, as well as a pleasing taste.

AMERICAN VELVET.

(For a party of four.)

Use a large fancy glass.

1 pint of champagne (Pommery Sec).

1 pint of Guinness stout.

Fill the glass half full with porter, the balance with champagne.

Mix slowly with a spoon, and serve.

26

One of the good ones, where the cost is not to be considered, and the best of ingredients should be used.

SLOE GIN PUNCH.

Use a mixing glass.

1 spoonful of sugar dissolved in a little seltzer water.
1 spoonful of raspberry syrup.
1½ wine glass of Sloe gin.
Juice of half a lime.
1 piece of pineapple.
3 or 4 blackberries.
2 or 3 dashes of benedictine.
Fill the glass with fine ice, shake well, decorate with fruit in season, and serve with straws.

JOHN COLLINS.

Use a mixing glass.

½ spoonful of sugar.
Juice of one whole lemon.
3 or 4 small lumps of ice.
1 wine glass of Holland gin.

Fill the glass with seltzer water, spoon well, and serve.

This drink must be consumed by the customer as soon as mixed, in order not to let the foam run over the top of the glass.

CATAWBA COBBLER.

Use a mixing glass.

1 teaspoonful of sugar dissolved in a little seltzer water.

1 slice of orange.

1 slice of pineapple.

Fill up one-half the glass with fine ice, the balance with Catawba wine, spoon well, dress with fruit, and serve with straws.

For a delicious mixture that is almost non-alcoholic this is the acme of perfection.

ST. CROIX CRUSTA.

Use a mixing glass.

Peel a clean lemon in one long string; place peel in wine glass so it will line the entire inside.

Dip the edge of glass and lemon peel in powdered sugar and mix as follows:

3 or 4 dashes of orchard syrup.

1 dash bitters (Angostura).

½ glass of fine ice.

1 small dash of lemon juice.

2 dashes of maraschino.

1 wine glass of St. Croix rum.

Mix well and strain into wine glass, ornament with fruit in season, and serve.

WHISKEY COBBLER.

Use a mixing glass.

½ teaspoonful of sugar dissolved in a little water.

2 slices of orange.

1 or 2 dashes of benedictine.

1½ wine glass of whiskey.

Fill the glass with fine ice, spoon well, dress with fruit, and serve with straws.

MONTE CARLO PUNCH.

Use a punch glass.

Juice of one whole orange.

1 spoonful of sugar.

1 pony glass of brandy.

29

1 or 2 dashes of benedictine.

Add fine shaved ice and fill the glass with claret.

Spoon well, add spray of mint, fruit in season, and serve with straws.

This punch was originally prepared at Monte Carlo, the world-renowned gambling resort, and immediately became popular with the habitués, and the formula was brought to the United States by an American gentleman, and it has since become extremely popular with the members of the most exclusive clubs in the country.

CREAM FIZZ.

Use a mixing glass.

½ spoonful of sugar.

3 or 4 dashes of lemon juice.

½ pony glass of pure cream.

1 wine glass of Maple gin.

Fill up the glass with fine ice.

Shake well, strain into a fizz glass, fill with seltzer water, and serve.

30

ST. CHARLES PUNCH.

Use a punch glass.

1 spoonful of sugar dissolved in a little seltzer.

2 or 3 dashes of lime juice.

1 pony glass of brandy (Hennessey).

1 wine glass of port wine.

½ pony glass of orange curacoa.

Fill the glass with fine ice, mix well with spoon, ornament with fruits in season, and serve with straws.

This punch was first served at the St. Charles Hotel at New Orleans, La., and is an extreme favorite with Southern people.

GIN FIZZ.

Use a mixing glass.

1 spoonful of sugar dissolved well in a little seltzer water.

3 dashes of lemon juice.

½ glass of fine ice.

1 wine glass of Tom gin.

Shake well, strain into a fizz glass, fill with seltzer water, and serve.

31

OLD-FASHIONED WHISKEY
COCKTAIL

Use a whiskey glass.

1 lump of loaf sugar dissolved in 1-3 glass of water.

2 or 3 dashes of bitters (Angostura).

1 small lump of ice.

½ wine glass of whiskey.

Twist a piece of lemon peel and drop it in the glass. Mix well with a spoon, and serve.

This mixture is called for very much by connoisseurs, and should always be mixed with loaf sugar.

WHISKEY FIZZ.

Use a mixing glass.

1 spoonful of sugar dissolved in a little seltzer water.

2 or 3 dashes of lemon juice.

1 wine glass of whiskey.

Fill up the glass with fine ice.

Shake well, strain into a fizz glass, fill with seltzer water, and serve.

32

RUM AND MOLASSES.

Use a whiskey glass.

Pour a small quantity of rum into it to cover the bottom of the glass.

Then take a spoonful of black molasses and place it in the glass, and hand the bottle of rum to the customer to help himself.

This drink is considered very good for a cold, or to prevent la grippe.

SLOE GIN FIZZ.

Use a mixing glass.

½ spoonful of sugar dissolved in a little seltzer water.

3 dashes of lemon juice.

½ glass of fine ice.

1 wine glass of Sloe gin.

Shake well, strain into a fizz glass, fill with seltzer, and serve.

STATE HOUSE PUNCH.

Use a punch glass.

1 spoonful of sugar dissolved in a little water or seltzer.

2 or 3 dashes of lemon juice.

33

½ glass of Mount Vernon whiskey.

1 pony glass of Jamaica rum.

Fill the glass with fine ice, mix well with spoon, decorate with orange, pineapple, berries, etc., top it off with claret, and serve with straws.

This punch derived its name from the fact that it was served in the first-class hostelries near the Massachusetts State House at Boston, and at once became very popular with the legislators.

ST. CROIX RUM FIZZ.

Use a mixing glass.

1 spoonful of sugar dissolved in a little seltzer water.

2 or 3 dashes of lemon juice.

1 wine glass of St. Croix rum.

Fill up the glass with shaved ice.

Shake well, strain into a fizz glass, fill with seltzer water, and serve.

BLACK JACK.

Use a small bar glass.

1 wine glass of St. Croix or Jamaica rum.

1 teaspoonful of black molasses.

If called for in summer, mix in a little

34

water and fine ice; if in the winter, fill the
glass with hot water, grate a little nutmeg
on top, and serve.

TOM COLLINS.

Use a mixing glass.

1 spoonful of sugar.

Juice of one whole lemon.

2 or 3 small lumps of ice.

1 wine glass of Tom gin.

Fill the glass with plain soda, spoon well
but slowly, and serve.

In serving this drink do not let it stand; if
so, the foam will run over the top of the
glass.

MEDFORD RUM FIZZ.

Use a mixing glass.

1 spoonful of sugar dissolved in a little
seltzer water.

2 or 3 dashes of lemon juice.

1 wine glass of Medford rum.

Fill up the glass with fine ice.

Shake well, strain into a fizz glass, fill with
seltzer water, and serve.

35

BRANDY STRAIGHT.

Use a whiskey glass.

Put a piece of ice in the glass, and let the customer serve himself from the bottle, with plain soda water on the side.

Whiskey Straight and Gin Straight are served in the same way, with ice water on the side.

BRANDY AND GUM.

Use a whiskey glass.

1 or 2 dashes of gum.

1 or 2 small lumps of ice.

Place a bar spoon in the glass, and hand this, with a bottle of brandy, to the customer to help himself.

Whiskey and gin are served in the same manner.

MISS LIBERTY.

Use a fancy stem glass.

Peel an orange in one long, narrow string; twist the same in cork-screw fashion; then place in centre of the glass, with one end protruding over top of glass; surround with fine

36

crystal ice, well packed. Fill the glass 1-3 parfait d'amour, 1-3 maraschino, and fill with creme de violette. Serve with straw.

Discovered at a collation served at Washington in honor/ of representative officers of the army and navy, and voted by them invincible.

BLUE BLAZER.

Use two mugs with handles.

½ pony glass gum syrup.
1 wine glass Scotch whiskey.

Mix well with a little hot water, then ignite the liquid and pour rapidly from one mug to the other three or four times, which will give the appearance of a stream of fire. Grate a little nutmeg on top, and serve in one of the mugs originally used, as it will retain the heat.

A great favorite with bartenders who are experts and can handle the mugs in such manner as to give the appearance of a pyrotechnical display, and thus show their dexterity in the art of mixology.

37

CLARET COBBLER.

Use a mixing glass.

1 teaspoonful of sugar dissolved in a little seltzer water.

1 or 2 slices of orange.

1 or 2 slices of pineapple.

2 wine glasses of claret wine.

Fill the glass with fine ice, spoon well, dress with fruit; serve with straw.

BRANDY FIZZ.

Use a mixing glass.

1 spoonful of sugar.

2 or 3 dashes of lemon juice dissolved in a little seltzer water.

1 wine glass of brandy (Hennessey).

Fill the glass with fine ice, shake well, strain into a fizz glass, fill up with seltzer, and serve.

SHANDY GAFF.

Use large ale glass.

Fill the glass half full of old ale. Fill the the other half with ginger ale; stir well with a spoon, and serve.

A mild and exhilarating drink, effervescent in a slight measure, and pleasing to the taste.

BRANDY FLOAT.

Use a pony glass.

Fill the glass with brandy (Hennessey). Cover it with a whiskey glass tightly together, and turn them over quickly so the pony glass will remain upside down in the whiskey glass. Then half fill the whiskey glass with plain soda or seltzer; take out the pony glass slowly, so the brandy will float on the top.

BRANDY AND GINGER ALE.

Use large thin bar glass.

1 piece of clean ice.
1 wine glass of brandy (Hennessey).
Fill the glass with Belfast ginger ale.
A mild-tasting mixture, but deceiving in consequences if indulged in with impunity.

39

APOLLINARIS LEMONADE.

Use a mixing glass.

1 spoonful of sugar.

6 or 7 dashes of lemon juice.

Fill the glass with fine ice, the balance with Apollinaris water. Stir well with spoon, and serve with straws.

NEW ENGLAND RUM TODDY.

Use medium size bar glass.

½ spoonful of sugar dissolved in a little water.

1 small lump of ice.

Twist a piece of lemon peel in the glass.

1 wine glass of New England rum.

Serve with a small bar spoon.

It is conceded by many that this old timer was originally landed from the Mayflower at Plymouth Rock by the Pilgrim Fathers, and was the real means of conciliating the native Indians.

COCKTAIL FRAPPÉ.

Use a mixing glass.

2 or 3 dashes of gum syrup.

1 light dash of Angostura bitters.

2-3 jigger of whiskey.

Fill up the glass with fine shaved ice. Shake with a shaker until the outside of the shaker is white with frost, strain into a straight bar glass, twist a piece of lemon peel on top, and serve.

Manhattan and Martini Cocktail should be made the same way, except using orange bitters.

CLARET LEMONADE.

Use a mixing glass.

1 spoonful of sugar.
3 or 4 dashes of lemon juice.
Fill the glass with fine ice, the balance with water. Shake well with a shaker, decorate with fruit in season, and top it off with claret, and serve with straws.

CREME DE MENTHE.

Use a cocktail glass.

Take the glass and pack it with very fine ice.

Fill the glass with creme de menthe, and serve with small straws.

41

In case you are asked for a Creme de
Menthe Frappé, put the above ingredients
in a large bar glass; fill the glass with fine
ice; shake well until the outside of the
shaker is white with frost, strain into a cocktail glass, and serve.

REMSEN COOLER.

Use large thin bar glass.

Peel the rind of a lemon and place it in the
side of the glass.

1 piece of clean ice.

1 wine glass of Honeysuckle gin.

Fill the glass with imported club soda, stir
slowly with a spoon, and serve.

Scotch whiskey may be used if preferable
to the taste.

BRANDY FLIP.

Use a mixing glass.

1 spoonful of sugar.

1 fresh egg.

1 wine glass of brandy (Hennessey).

1 pony glass of pure cream.

Fill the glass with fine ice, shake well,
strain into a fancy stem glass, grate a little
nutmeg on top, and serve.

APPLE WHISKEY SOUR.

Use a mixing glass.

1 spoonful of sugar.

2 or 3 dashes of lemon juice.

1 squirt of seltzer water; dissolve well.

½ glass of fine ice.

1 wine glass of apple whiskey (sometimes called cider brandy).

Spoon well, strain into a sour glass, put in fruit, and serve.

As is known to many, any mixture of which apple whiskey forms a component part is the offspring of some part of the state of New Jersey, and the foregoing is no exception.

ROMAN PUNCH.

Use a punch glass.

1 spoonful of sugar dissolved in a little plain soda.

2 or 3 dashes of lime juice.

Juice of 1 whole orange.

2 dashes of curacoa.

½ wine glass of brandy (Hennessey).

½ pony glass of Jamaica rum.

Fill the glass with fine ice, mix well with

43

spoon, dash with claret wine, decorate with fruit in season, and serve with straws.

The standard punch for parties, receptions, etc., and very palatable.

HOW TO SERVE TOM AND JERRY.

Use a Tom and Jerry mug.

2 spoonfuls of batter.
1 wine glass of brandy (Hennessey).
1 pony glass of Jamaica rum.

Fill the mug with hot water, or hot milk; spoon well, then pour the mixture from one mug to the other four or five times, grate a little nutmeg on top, and serve.

HIGH BALL.

Use a fizz glass.

1 or 2 small lumps of ice.
1 wine glass of Plymouth gin.

Fill the glass with ice cold syphon seltzer.

If customer requires whiskey or brandy, mix in the same manner.

This, without doubt, is the blue ribbon long drink in which an alcoholic fluid is a factor.

44

HOT EGG NOG.

Use a mixing glass.

1 fresh egg.
2 spoonfuls of sugar.
½ wine glass of Cognac.
½ wine glass of Jamaica rum.

Fill the glass with boiling hot milk, stirring contents well while adding the milk; grate nutmeg on top, and serve.

This drink will be found very beneficial to delicate persons, as it is not only a tonic, but strengthening and, if used regularly, will assist very materially in building up the system.

IMPERIAL RUM PUNCH.

4 quarts of Apollinaris water.
1 pint of claret.
3 pints of Jamaica rum.
1 pint of Medford rum.
1 pint of brandy.
1½ pounds of sugar.
Juice of 10 lemons.
1 pineapple pared and sliced.
4 oranges sliced.
1 wine glass of curacoa.
1 gin glass of raspberry syrup.

45

Put in a punch bowl and pack in ice; add
berries in season. Serve with ladle in small
punch glasses.

EVENING DAISY.

Use a mixing glass.

¾ glass of fine shaved ice.
2 or 3 dashes of lime juice.
1 spoonful of sugar.
3 or 4 dashes of absinthe.
White of one egg.
1 wine glass of Irish whiskey.
Shake well, strain into a wine glass, and
serve.

HORSE'S NECK.

Use a large thin bar glass.

Peel a lemon in one long string, place in a
glass with one end projecting over the edge
of glass; add a large piece of clean ice, and
fill the glass with imported ginger ale.

A temperance drink which is refreshing
and has an appetizing and inviting appearance.

BOTTLE OF MARTINI COCKTAIL.

Use bar shaker for mixing.

1 pony glass of orange bitters.
½ pony glass of maraschino.
Half fill the shaker with fine ice.
1-3 bottle of French vermuth.
2-3 bottle of Tom gin.

Mix well with spoon, strain into a full quart bottle, cork and label.

Always use a dark-colored bottle when mixing cocktails for a party.

This is supposed to be a very dry cocktail.

Ice should always be used in making bottled cocktails.

BRANDY SANGAREE.

Use a mixing glass.

Half fill glass with fine ice.
½ wine glass of water.
1 spoonful of sugar.
1 glass of brandy.

Shake well, strain into a stem glass, grate nutmeg on top, and serve.

47

BOTTLE WHISKEY COCKTAIL.

Use bar shaker for mixing.

Fill the shaker one-third full of fine ice.

½ wine glass of gum syrup.

1 pony of benedictine.

½ pony glass of bitters (Angostura).

Pour in one quart of good whiskey; mix well with long bar spoon, strain into a quart bottle, cork and label, and your preparation is ready for delivery to customer.

EGG SOUR.

Use a mixing glass.

2 spoonfuls of sugar.

2 dashes of lemon juice.

1 pony glass of curacoa.

1 glass of brandy (Hennessey).

1 yolk of an egg.

¾ glass of finely shaved ice.

Shake well and strain into a fancy stem glass.

The above might almost be classed as a prescription instead of a mixed drink, but can be obtained at well regulated and exclusive cafes where competent dispensers are employed.

48

BOTTLE MANHATTAN COCKTAIL.

Use bar shaker for mixing.

½ wine glass of gum syrup.
½ pony glass of bitters (Angostura).
1 pony glass of orange curacoa.
Half fill the shaker with fine ice.
1-3 bottle of vermuth.
2-3 bottle of good whiskey.
Stir well with long bar spoon, strain into a full quart bottle, and cork.

Place an attractive label on the bottle, and you will have a bottle of cocktail that will please your most exacting patron.

PORTER SANGAREE.

Use a mixing glass.

2 spoonfuls of sugar dissolved in water.
3 or 4 lumps of ice.
Fill the glass with porter, stir well, and grate nutmeg on top.

BRANDY SCAFFA.

Use pousse cafe glass.

¼ glass of raspberry syrup.
¼ glass of maraschino.

49

$\frac{1}{4}$ glass of chartreuse (green).

Top off with brandy, and serve.

One of the pretty ones, with a rainbow effect, which, if properly prepared, is very attractive.

WHISKEY SMASH.

Use a mixing glass.

1 spoonful of sugar.

1 wine glass of seltzer water.

2 or 3 sprigs of fresh mint; dissolve well until the essence of the mint is extracted.

Half fill the glass with fine ice.

1 wine glass of whiskey.

Mix well with a spoon, strain into a fancy stem glass, put in fruit, and serve.

BRANDY CRUSTA.

Take a lemon and cut off the ends, peel off the whole rind, and place it inside of a wine glass; rub a slice of lemon around the edge of the glass, dip the glass in powdered sugar, then take your mixing glass and mix as follows:

50

2 or 3 dashes of gum syrup.

1 or 2 dashes of bitters (Angostura).

1 or 2 dashes of lime juice.

2 dashes of white curacoa.

1 wine glass of brandy (Hennessey).

Fill the glass with fine ice, mix well with a spoon, strain into a fancy stem glass, dress with fruit, and serve.

SWISS ESS.

Use a mixing glass.

½ spoonful of sugar.

1 or 2 dashes of lime juice.

2 or 3 dashes of absinthe.

1 fresh egg (white only).

½ glass of brandy (Hennessey).

2 or 3 dashes of maraschino.

Fill the glass with fine ice, shake well with a shaker, strain into a sour glass, fill with syphon seltzer, and serve.

A combination which eradicates that allgone feeling, and at the same time is healing to the stomach, but should be taken in moderation, as an excessive use of any form of cordial is injurious.

51

HOT LEMONADE.

Use a mixing glass.

1 spoonful of sugar.

5 or 6 dashes of lemon juice.

Fill the glass with hot water, spoon well, and serve.

This is one of the best known preventives for a cold if taken at its incipiency, but should only be taken immediately before retiring, as it opens the pores of the entire body.

BRANDY SMASH.

Use a mixing glass.

1 spoonful of sugar dissolved in small quantity of mineral water.

Crush 3 or 4 sprays of mint until essence is extracted.

1 wine glass of brandy (Hennessey).

Fill the glass with fine ice, stir well, and strain into a sour glass; add slice of orange, lemon and fruit in season.

PORT WINE SANGAREE.

Use a sour glass.

1 or 2 lumps of ice.

2 spoonfuls of sugar.

Fill the glass with port wine, stir well, and grate a little nutmeg on top.

HOT APPLE TODDY.

Use large hot water glass.

$\frac{1}{2}$ spoonful of sugar.

$\frac{1}{2}$ of a small baked apple.

1 wine glass of apple jack.

Fill the glass with hot water, mix well with a spoon, grate a little nutmeg on top, and serve with small bar spoon.

One of the best to break up a cold, if taken at its inception.

BRANDY JULEP.

Use a mixing glass.

2 spoonfuls of sugar.

$\frac{1}{2}$ wine glass of mineral water.

Crush 3 or 4 sprigs of mint until essence is extracted.

1 wine glass of brandy (Hennessey).

53

Fill the glass with shaved ice, and shake well. Ornament with sprays of mint, sliced orange, and fruit in season, sprinkle a little pulverized sugar on top, and add a dash of Jamaica rum.

This stimulant is an extremely exhilarating one, and a great favorite with the élite of the South, where it has been in vogue for many years.

SHERRY WINE PUNCH.

Use a punch glass.

1 or 2 dashes of raspberry syrup.
½ spoonful of sugar.
1-3 wine glass of seltzer water.
2 or 3 dashes of lemon juice.
1½ wine glass of sherry wine.

Fill the glass with fine ice, shake well with shaker, dress the top with fruit in season, and serve with straws.

SHERRY WINE SANGAREE.

Use a sour glass.

2 spoonfuls of sugar.
1 or 2 lumps of ice.
1 wine glass of sherry wine.
Stir well and add a little nutmeg.

54

SHERRY CHICKEN.

Use a mixing glass.

1 spoonful of sugar.

1½ wine glass of sherry wine.

1 fresh egg.

½ glass of fine ice.

Shake well, strain into a fancy stem glass, grate a little nutmeg on top, and serve.

A delicious mixture of nourishing ingredients, which is harmless in its consequences.

PORT WINE PUNCH.

Use a punch glass.

½ spoonful of raspberry syrup.

½ spoonful of sugar dissolved in a little seltzer water.

2 or 3 dashes of maraschino.

2 or 3 dashes of lemon juice.

Fill the glass with fine ice.

1½ wine glass of port wine.

Spoon well, decorate with fruit in season, and serve with straws.

A drink very popular with the fair sex who are very moderate drinkers, as it is sweet and very palatable.

55

Historic Cookbooks of the World

SHERRY WINE EGG NOG.

Use a mixing glass.

1 spoonful of sugar.

1 fresh egg.

1½ wine glass of sherry wine.

1 pony glass of brandy (Hennessey).

½ glass of fine ice.

Fill the glass with milk, shake well, strain into a large bar glass, grate a little nutmeg on top, and serve with straws.

Unsurpassed as an invigorator, not only for a short time as many are, but it will stand by you for a considerable period.

BRANDY SPLIT.

Use a medium thin bar glass.

1 pony glass of brandy.

1 or 2 small lumps of ice.

1 bottle of club soda.

Fill up the glass, and divide equally in two star champagne glasses.

A good bracer to start a man to business in the morning, with his pipes cleaned, and courage under his vest.

56

HOW TO MIX TOM AND JERRY.

Take 18 strictly fresh eggs.

Break the same into two punch bowls, the whites in one, and the yolks in the other.

Then take an egg beater and beat the whites of the eggs to a stiff froth; then add 2 spoonfuls of sugar and mix thoroughly.

The yolks of the eggs are then to be beaten until they are as thin as water, after which mix the yolks and whites together and add sufficient powdered sugar to have the mixture attain the consistency of a light batter. Stir the mixture from time to time to prevent the eggs from separating.

GIN RICKEY.

Use a sour glass.

Squeeze the juice of one lime into it.

1 small lump of ice.

1 wine glass of Plymouth gin.

Fill the glass with syphon seltzer, and serve with small bar spoon.

This drink was devised by the late Colonel Rickey of Kentucky, whose fame as a congenial friend and dispenser of hospitality, as well as a judge of appetizing edibles and liquid refreshments, is world-wide, and it is universally conceded that for a drink containing an alcoholic ingredient it is the most cooling and refreshing beverage known.

CLARET FLIP.

Use a mixing glass.

2 bar spoonfuls of sugar.
1 fresh egg.
1½ wine glass of claret.
2-3 glass full of shaved ice.
Shake thoroughly, and strain into a fancy bar glass, adding a little nutmeg on the top.

BRUNSWICK.

Use a mixing glass.

1 spoonful of powdered sugar.
1 fresh cold egg.
Half fill the glass with fine ice, fill up the balance with milk; shake up well, strain into a large bar glass, grate a little nutmeg on top, and serve with straws.

The above is a good substitute for a breakfast for persons whose appetite has abandoned them and who are feverish and require something strengthening.

58

MANHATTAN COCKTAIL.

Use a mixing glass.

Half fill with fine ice.

1 dash of Angostura bitters.

½ wine glass of whiskey.

½ wine glass of vermuth.

Stir with spoon, strain into a cocktail glass, put in a cherry or olive, and serve.

One that is a dear and lasting friend to the Bohemians, and probably called for more extensively than any other morning favorite.

RUSTY IKE.

Use a rickey glass.

Squeeze the juice of one whole lime into it.

1 or 2 small lumps of ice.

1 wine glass of Medford or New England rum.

Fill the glass with ginger ale, and serve with a small bar spoon.

APPLE WHISKEY COCKTAIL.

Use a mixing glass.

2 dashes of gum syrup.

1 dash of Angostura bitters.

59

¾ wine glass of apple whiskey.

Spoon well and strain into a cocktail glass, twist a piece of lemon peel on top, and serve.

This drink is much called for in the state of New Jersey, the home of apple jack.

DALY'S ROYAL FIZZ.

Use a mixing glass.

½ fill the glass with fine ice.

2 or 3 dashes of lemon juice.

2 or 3 dashes of lime juice.

1 spoonful of powdered sugar.

1 pony of cream.

1 wine glass of Tom gin.

1 whole egg.

Shake well in shaker and strain into a fizz glass; fill with cold syphon seltzer, spoon well, and serve.

This fizz was devised by Mr. Daly after exhaustive research and has been highly commended by every one having had the good fortune to imbibe one, and its popularity is growing daily wherever it has been introduced.

60

SODA COCKTAIL.

Use a mixing glass.

3 lumps of ice.
6 dashes of Angostura bitters.
1 or 2 slices of orange.

Fill up the glass with seltzer drawn from a syphon; place a spoon on top of the glass filled with pulverized sugar, for the customer to put in himself.

In mixing be very careful not to let the foam run over the top of the glass.

An early morning concoction to alleviate a headache and settle the stomach.

U. C. T. LEMONADE.

Use a mixing glass.

1 large teaspoonful of sugar.
6 or 7 dashes of lemon juice.

Fill up the glass with ice, the balance with water; shake up well in a shaker, dash with Jamaica rum, and serve with straws.

This drink is called for by members of the United Commercial Travelers' Association throughout the country, and, as it was named in honor of their association, they are extremely partial to it.

61

CHAMPAGNE COCKTAIL.

Use a champagne goblet.

Take a lump of sugar.

3 dashes of Angostura bitters.

1 small lump of ice.

Fill the goblet with wine, stir with a spoon, twist a piece of lemon on top, and serve.

½ pint of wine is suitable for one cocktail.

This is the cream of all morning cocktails, and under no circumstances should anything but the best of imported champagne be used, and the drink should be ice-cold and consumed slowly.

EARLY BIRD.

Use star champagne glass.

Fill ¾ full of syphon seltzer.

Add 3 dashes of absinthe.

Float small quantity of brandy on top, and serve.

TUXEDO COCKTAIL.

Use a mixing glass.

Half fill with fine ice.

2 dashes of orange bitters.

2 dashes of maraschino.

½ wine glass of French vermuth.
½ wine glass of maple gin.
Spoon well and strain into a cocktail glass; put in a cherry and twist a piece of lemon peel on top, and serve.

SUNNY SIDE LEMONADE.

Use a mixing glass.

1 large spoonful of sugar.
5 or 6 dashes of lemon juice.
Fill up the glass with fine ice, the balance with water; shake well in a shaker, dash with port wine, ornament with fruit in season, and serve with straws.

TRILBY COCKTAIL.

Use a mixing glass.

Fill with fine ice.
2 dashes of orange bitters.
1 dash of absinthe.
2 dashes of parfait d'amour.
½ wine glass of Scotch whiskey.
½ wine glass of French vermuth.
Spoon well, strain into a cocktail glass, put in a cherry, twist a piece of orange peel on top, and serve.

63

HOT SCOTCH WHISKEY PUNCH.

Use hot whiskey glass.

1 lump of loaf sugar.

Half fill the glass with hot water.

Dissolve the sugar.

1 slice of lemon.

Fill the glass with Scotch whiskey.

Stir with spoon, grate a little nutmeg on top, and serve.

IMPERIAL COCKTAIL.

Use a mixing glass.

Half fill with fine ice.

1 or 2 dashes of aromatic bitters.

1 dash of maraschino.

½ wine glass of French vermuth.

½ wine glass of Plymouth gin.

Spoon well, strain into a cocktail glass, put in an olive, and serve.

The above is very popular with Europeans of the better class, particularly the French, who are extremely fond of cordials of all descriptions.

FORMULA FOR MAKING A SIMPLE SYRUP, COMMONLY CALLED "GUM."

Take two pounds of rock candy or 2½ pounds of loaf sugar and place in one quart of water and allow to simmer over a slow fire until thorougly dissolved (care should be taken not to allow it to come to a boil, as the gum in that event is apt to spoil); filter through a clean piece of cheese cloth, and your gum is ready for use.

HOT MILK PUNCH.

Use a mixing glass.

1 teaspoonful of sugar.

1 wine glass of brandy (Hennessey).

½ wine glass of St. Croix rum.

Fill the glass with hot milk, stir well with spoon while filling; grate a little nutmeg on top, and serve.

RHINE WINE PUNCH.

Use a punch glass.

1 large spoonful of sugar dissolved in a little seltzer.

2 or 3 dashes of lemon juice.

Fill up the glass with fine shaved ice, the

balance with Rhine wine; mix well with a spoon, decorate top with fruit in season, and serve with straws.

A great favorite with representatives of Germany in foreign countries who wish to show their affiliation for the Fatherland.

PORT WINE COCKTAIL.

Use a mixing glass.

Half fill with fine ice.

2 dashes of aromatic bitters.

1 dash of benedictine.

1 wine glass of port wine.

Spoon well, strain into a cocktail glass, twist a piece of orange peel on top, and serve.

Another weak one, but very beneficial, and will not result in a headache.

COFFEE COBBLER.

Use extra large bar glass.

6 or 7 lumps of ice.

1 spoonful of sugar.

Mix together a pony of cream and a pony of brandy; pour into the bar glass, then fill the glass with black coffee, spoon well, and serve.

66

The foregoing is practically the same formula employed in the tea cobbler, merely the ingredients being changed to suit the taste of persons impartial to the flavor of rum and tea.

HAMPSHIRE MAID.

Use mixing glass.

Pony glass of claret.
Pony glass of Rhine wine.
Add shaved ice and shake well, add 4 dashes of creme de menthe; pour into thin bar glass and fill with club soda.

This is one of the mild, tart drinks most favorably considered at the Hampshire Hotel, which is almost exclusively patronized by young ladies from the various seminaries of New England.

ABSINTHE COCKTAIL.
"American Style."

Use a mixing glass.

Fill with fine ice.
2 dashes of gum syrup.
1 dash of Angostura bitters.

1 dash of anisette.
1 wine glass of absinthe.
Shake until the outside of the shaker is white with frost; strain into a cocktail glass, twist a piece of lemon peel on top, and serve.

TEA COBBLER.

Use extra large bar glass.

6 or 7 lumps of cracked ice.
1 spoonful of powdered sugar.
Juice of one whole lemon.
Fill the glass with black tea, add a dash of Jamaica rum, spoon well, and serve.

This makes a delightful accompaniment with a light noonday lunch, and should be served thoroughly cold.

OYSTER COCKTAIL.

Use a medium wine glass.

3 dashes of catsup.
2 medium-sized oysters.
Salt and pepper to season; one dash of lime juice, and serve.

RUM PUNCH.

Use a punch glass.

1 teaspoonful of sugar dissolved in a little water.

The juice of one lime.

1½ glasses of Medford rum.

Fill the glass with fine ice.

1 dash of St. Croix rum.

Stir well with spoon, dress with fruit, and serve with straws.

MARTINI COCKTAIL.

Use a mixing glass.

Half fill with fine ice.

2 dashes of orange bitters.

½ wine glass of Tom gin.

½ wine glass of vermuth.

Spoon well and strain into a cocktail glass; put in an olive, and serve.

GIN PUNCH.

Use a punch glass.

1 teaspoonful of sugar dissolved in a little water or seltzer.

½ teaspoonful of raspberry syrup.

2 or 3 dashes of lemon juice.

1½ wine glasses of Holland gin.

2 dashes of benedictine.

Fill the glass with fine ice, stir well with a spoon, dress the top with fruit, and serve with straws.

HOT GIN SLING.

Use hot whiskey glass.

1 lump of loaf sugar.

Half fill the glass with hot water to dissolve the sugar.

Fill up the glass with Holland gin, and serve.

CLARET PUNCH.

Use a punch glass.

1 teaspoonful of powdered sugar.

1 or 2 dashes of lemon juice.

Pack the glass with fine ice, pour in the claret and shake well, decorate with fruit in season, and serve with straws.

One of the oldest as well as the most delicious punches, which has many old friends and is constantly making new ones.

70

VERMUTH COCKTAIL.

Use a mixing glass.

Half fill with fine ice.
2 dashes of orange bitters.
1 dash of benedictine.
1 wine glass of vermuth.
Spoon well, strain into a cocktail glass, put in a cherry or olive, and serve.

Most soothing to the nerves and invigorating to a large degree, as well as pleasing to the palate.

STOMACH LINING.

Use small bar glass.

¾ fill with hot clam broth.
Add lime water to fill glass, and serve hot.

Clam juice is acknowledged by leading physicians to be the most healing article for a weak stomach and can be retained and digested by the most delicate persons.

OLIVE COCKTAIL.

Use a mixing glass.

Half fill with fine ice.
1 or 2 dashes of gum syrup.

1 dash of Angostura bitters.
1 wine glass of Plymouth gin.
2 dashes of absinthe.
Spoon well, strain into cocktail glass, put in olive, and serve.

MARBLE WALL.

Use a gin glass.

Pony of whiskey.
Fill glass with Rhine wine.
This is an improvement on the old-fashioned stone fence and is much more delicate in flavor.

JOCKEY CLUB COCKTAIL.

Use a mixing glass.

Half fill with fine ice.
2 dashes of gum syrup.
1 dash of Angostura bitters.
$\frac{1}{2}$ wine glass of Jamaica rum.
$\frac{1}{2}$ wine glass of vermuth.
1 dash of kümmel.
Spoon well, strain into a cocktail glass, put in an olive, twist the peel of a lemon on top, and serve.

In great demand wherever followers of the turf congregate, and a decoction which does not require a handicap.

72

SAUTERNE PUNCH.

Use a large punch glass.

1 teaspoonful of sugar.
1 slice of lemon.
1 slice of orange.
1 slice of pineapple.

Fill the glass with fine ice, pour in sauterne.

Mix well, dress with fruit, and serve with straws.

The nonpareil running mate to a hammock in a shady nook on a hot summer's day, when the vigor lost through perspiration should be replaced by a fitting substitute.

BRANDY SLING.

Use hot whiskey glass.
1 lump of loaf sugar.

Half fill the glass with hot water and dissolve the sugar.

Fill the glass with brandy, and serve.

ROOSTER COCKTAIL.

Use a mixing glass.

Half fill with fine ice.
2 dashes of aromatic bitters.

73

1 dash of benedictine.

1 wine glass of London Dry Burrough gin.

Spoon well, strain into a cocktail glass, put in an olive, and serve.

HOT RUM.

Use hot whiskey glass.

1 or 2 lumps of sugar.

Half fill the glass with hot water and dissolve the sugar.

Fill the glass with rum, grate a little nutmeg on top, and serve.

HOT IRISH WHISKEY PUNCH.

Use hot whiskey glass.

1 lump of loaf sugar.

Half fill the glass with boiling water.

Dissolve the sugar, fill up with Irish whiskey.

1 dash of lemon juice.

Stir with spoon, grate a little nutmeg on top, and serve.

74

TURF COCKTAIL.

Use a mixing glass.

Half fill with fine ice.

2 dashes of orange bitters.

2 dashes of maraschino.

½ wine glass of French vermuth.

½ wine glass of honeysuckle gin.

Spoon well, strain into a cocktail glass, put in a cherry, and serve.

HOT SPICED RUM.

Use hot whiskey glass.

1 lump of loaf sugar.

Half fill the glass with hot water.

Dissolve the sugar.

½ teaspoonful of allspice.

Fill up the glass with rum.

Grate a little nutmeg on top, and serve.

The most aromatic decoction known to the art of mixology, and as pleasing to the taste as it is stimulating to the system.

HOT WHISKEY PUNCH.

Use hot whiskey glass.

1 lump of loaf sugar.

Half fill the glass with hot water and dissolve the sugar.

75

1 dash of lemon juice.

Fill up the glass with whiskey.

Grate a little nutmeg on top, and serve.

SARATOGA COCKTAIL.

Use a mixing glass.

Half fill with fine ice.

2 dashes of pineapple syrup.

2 dashes of orange bitters.

1 dash of maraschino.

¾ of a glass of brandy.

Spoon well, strain into a cocktail glass, put in a couple of strawberries when the fruit is in season, twist lemon peel on top, and serve.

A foster-brother to the full-fledged and full-dressed gamblers who patronize the famous Spa.

HOT SCOTCH WHISKEY SLING.

Use hot whiskey glass.

1 lump of loaf sugar.

Half fill the glass with hot water to dissolve the sugar.

Fill the glass with Scotch whiskey, and serve.

MARGUERITE COCKTAIL.

Use a mixing glass.

Half fill with fine ice.

2 dashes of orange bitters.

1 dash of orange curacoa.

½ wine glass of French vermuth.

½ wine glass of Plymouth gin.

Stir well with spoon, strain into a cocktail glass, twist a piece of lemon peel on top, and serve.

BRACER.

Use whiskey glass.

Elixir bromide potassium, 2 teaspoonfuls.

1 teaspoonful tincture gentian; fill the glass ¾ full of water, and serve.

The above, as the name implies, is a bracer and one that is appreciated by gentlemen who feel the effects of the preceding night's dinner, etc., and are looking for a useful friend in the morning.

GIN SOUR.

Use a mixing glass.

½ teaspoonful of sugar dissolved in a little seltzer.

2 or 3 dashes of lemon juice.

1 wine glass of Holland gin.

Half fill the glass with fine ice.

Spoon well, strain into a sour glass, put in fruit, and serve.

The best possible preparation to eradicate the fuz from a person's tongue after a night in Bohemia, where variety seemed the absorbing ambition.

RUM COCKTAIL.

Use a mixing glass.

2 or 3 dashes of gum syrup.

1 dash of bitters (Angostura).

1 wine glass of Medford rum.

Spoon well, strain into a cocktail glass, twist a piece of lemon peel on top, and serve.

MARASCHINO PUNCH.

Use a punch glass.

1 spoonful of sugar dissolved in a little seltzer.

1 wine glass of brandy (Hennessey).

2 dashes of lemon juice.

The juice of one orange.

78

1 pony glass of maraschino.

Fill the glass with fine ice, shake well, dress the top with fruit, and serve with straws.

Considered the real thing by members of the foreign legations in the United States.

HONEYSUCKLE GIN COCKTAIL.

Use a mixing glass.

Half fill with fine ice.

2 dashes of gum syrup.

1 dash of bitters (Angostura).

1 wine glass of honeysuckle gin.

Spoon well, strain into a cocktail glass, twist a piece of lemon peel on top, and serve.

COLLEGE DREAM.

Use a fancy sherry glass.

Half fill the glass with benedictine, drop in the yolk of one egg, fill up with pure cream, and serve. In serving this mixture the yolk of the egg must be fresh and cold.

The beau ideal of the college boys with a rugged constitution, and should be used sparingly by persons who are not gifted with a strong physique.

79

CURACOA PUNCH.

Use a punch glass.

1 teaspoonful of sugar dissolved in a little seltzer or water.

Juice of half a lime.

½ pony glass of orange curacoa.

1 wine glass of Jamaica rum.

Fill the glass with fine ice, stir well with a spoon, dress with orange, pineapple, berries, when in season, and serve with straws.

GLEE CLUB COCKTAIL.

Use a mixing glass.

Half fill with fine ice.

2 dashes of orange bitters.

1 dash of yellow chartreuse.

1 dash of maraschino.

1 wine glass of raspberry wine.

Spoon well, strain into a cocktail glass, put in a cherry, twist a piece of lemon peel on top, and serve.

ANGEL'S TIT.

Use a pousse cafe glass.

1-3 glass of raspberry syrup.

1-3 glass of creme yvette.

1-3 glass of pure cream.

Stick a toothpick into a cherry, lay the toothpick on the top of the glass so that the cherry will set into the cream, and serve.

One of the attractive ones which appeal to the eye, it being artistic in appearance, and withal is a palate tickler.

HOT SCOTCH WHISKEY SKIN.

Use hot whiskey glass.

1 lump of loaf sugar.

Half fill the glass with hot water and dissolve the sugar.

Fill up the glass with Scotch whiskey, twist a piece of lemon peel on top, and serve.

WHISKEY COCKTAIL.

Use a mixing glass.

Half fill with fine ice.

2 or 3 dashes of gum syrup.

1 dash of bitters (Angostura).

1 wine glass of whiskey.

Spoon well and strain into a cocktail glass, put in a cherry or olive, and serve.

So generally known for a long time that comment seems entirely unnecessary, but it undoubtedly still has a long life before it.

ST. CROIX SOUR.

Use a mixing glass.

$\frac{1}{2}$ teaspoonful of sugar dissolved in a little water or seltzer.

2 or 3 dashes of lemon juice.

1 wine glass of St. Croix rum.

Half fill the glass with fine ice.

Stir well with a spoon and strain into a sour glass, dress with fruit, and serve.

WHISKEY PUNCH.

Use a punch glass.

1 teaspoonful of sugar dissolved in a little water.

2 or 3 dashes of lemon juice.

$1\frac{1}{2}$ wine glass of whiskey.

Fill the glass with fine ice, mix well with a spoon, dress the top with fruit in season, and serve with straws.

82

HOT WHISKEY SKIN.

Use hot whiskey glass.

1 lump of sugar.

Half fill the glass with hot water, dissolve the sugar, then fill the glass with whiskey, twist a piece of lemon on top, and serve.

BRANDY COCKTAIL.

Use a mixing glass

Half fill with fine ice.

2 dashes of gum syrup.

1 dash of bitters (Angostura).

1 wine glass of brandy (Martel).

1 dash of benedictine.

Spoon well, strain into a cocktail glass, put in an olive or cherry, and serve.

BRANDY PUNCH.

Use a punch glass.

1 teaspoonful of sugar dissolved in a little seltzer water.

Juice of one lime.

1 dash of raspberry syrup.

1½ wine glass of brandy.

83

Fill the glass with fine ice and spoon well; put in two sprigs of mint, stems down; dash with Jamaica rum, ornament with orange, pineapple and berries, and serve with straws.

TOM GIN COCKTAIL.

Use a mixing glass.

Half fill with fine ice.
2 or 3 dashes of orange bitters.
1 dash of maraschino.
1 wine glass of Tom gin.
Spoon well, strain into a cocktail glass, put in cherry, and serve.

JAMAICA RUM SOUR.

Use a mixing glass.

$\frac{1}{2}$ teaspoonful of sugar dissolved in a little water or seltzer.
2 or 3 dashes of lemon juice.
1 wine glass of Jamaica rum.
Half fill the glass with fine ice.
Stir well with a spoon, strain into a sour glass, put in fruit, and serve.

WHITE MOUNTAIN.

Use a large bar glass.

1 bar spoonful of pulverized sugar.

1 fresh egg.

½ jigger of brandy.

½ jigger of port wine.

Half fill glass with fine ice and add milk to fill glass; shake well; strain into thin bar glass, adding nutmeg, and serve with straws.

The above is equivalent in consistency to a substantial meal and fully as satisfying.

MAPLE GIN COCKTAIL.

Use a mixing glass.

Half fill with fine ice.

2 dashes of orange bitters.

1 dash of benedictine.

1 wine glass of maple gin.

Spoon well, strain into a cocktail glass, put in an olive, twist a piece of lemon peel on top, and serve.

HOLLAND GIN COCKTAIL.

Use a mixing glass.

Half fill with fine ice.

2 dashes of gum syrup.

1 dash of bitters (Angostura).

1 wine glass of Holland gin.

Spoon well, strain into a cocktail glass, twist a piece of lemon peel on top, and serve.

FANCY BRANDY SOUR.

Use a mixing glass.

½ spoonful of sugar dissolved in a little seltzer water.

3 dashes of lemon juice.

1 wine glass of brandy (Hennessey).

Half fill the glass with fine ice, spoon well, strain into a sour glass, put in fruit, top off with claret, and serve.

SILVER FIZZ.

Use a mixing glass.

1 teaspoonful of sugar dissolved in a squirt of seltzer.

2 or 3 dashes of lemon juice.

1 wine glass of Tom gin.

1 fresh egg (white only).

Fill up the glass with shaved ice, shake well; strain into a fizz glass, fill up with seltzer, spoon well, and serve.

86

SHERRY WINE COCKTAIL.

Use a mixing glass.

Half fill with fine ice.

2 dashes of aromatic bitters.

1 dash of yellow chartreuse.

1 wine glass of sherry wine.

Spoon well, strain into a cocktail glass, put in a cherry, and serve.

SHERRY FLIP.

Use a mixing glass.

½ spoonful of sugar.

1 fresh egg.

1 pony of cream.

1 small bar glass of sherry wine.

Shake well in a shaker, strain into a fancy stem glass, grate a little nutmeg on top, and serve.

A smooth, nourishing mixture, invaluable to delicate persons; pleasing to the taste and highly invigorating.

WHISKEY DAISY.

Use a mixing glass.

½ teaspoonful of sugar.

2 or 3 dashes of lemon juice; dissolve

well in a squirt of seltzer.

½ pony glass of yellow chartreuse.

Fill the glass with shaved ice.

1 wine glass of good whiskey.

Stir well with spoon and strain into a fancy glass, decorate with fruit, and serve.

A daisy in fact as well as in name and a very smooth concoction.

MARCONI COCKTAIL.

Use a mixing glass.

½ jigger of Plymouth gin.

½ jigger of Italian vermuth.

Cracked ice.

1 piece of orange, which should be put in at the end.

In cutting the orange go deep enough to get some of the pulp, as the oil of the orange and the fruit together make a delightful blend; strain into a cocktail glass, and serve.

This drink was named after the renowned inventor, Signor Marconi, and is as modern as that gentleman's system of wireless telegraphy.

88

CHAMPAGNE COBBLER.

Use a champagne goblet.

1 pint of wine to two glasses.

½ teaspoonful of sugar.

½ wine glass of seltzer; stir well to dissolve the sugar.

2 slices of pineapple.

2 slices of orange.

Fill the glass with shaved ice, fill with champagne, stir very slowly, decorate the top with fruit, and serve with straws.

SELTZER LEMONADE.

Use a mixing glass.

1 large spoonful of sugar.

3 or 4 dashes of lemon juice.

Fill up the glass with fine ice and the balance with seltzer, spoon well, and serve with straws.

A cool and refreshing long drink, to which even our friend, Carrie Nation, could not take exception.

CHAMPAGNE JULEP.

Use a fancy stem glass.

Place one lump of sugar into the glass, add two sprigs of mint, then pour cham-

89

pagne slowly into the glass, stirring slowly
all the time; put in a slice of pineapple and
some raspberries, decorate the top in a
tasty manner, and serve.

KLONDIKE COCKTAIL.

Use a mixing glass.

Fill with fine ice.
2 dashes of orange bitters.
1 dash of benedictine.
1 wine glass of Tom gin.
Put in a small dash of eau de vie, squeeze
a piece of lemon into the glass, and serve.

A nugget which is sought after by
returned miners and prospectors from the
gold fields of Alaska who have struck it
rich, but have missed the luxuries unat-
tainable in that far-off region.

MILK AND SELTZER.

Use a medium size glass.

Half fill the glass with seltzer and the
balance with milk; always put the milk in
last, as it will save time, for if the milk is
put in first the foam will run over the top
of the glass.

90

This is a very soothing and refreshing drink and unsurpassed as a thirst quencher with a body to it.

PINK SOUR.

Use a mixing glass.

$\frac{1}{2}$ teaspoonful of sugar dissolved in a little seltzer.
2 dashes of lemon juice.
1 pony glass of St. Croix rum.
1 wine glass of brandy.
Half fill the glass with fine ice.
Spoon well, strain into a sour glass; add 3 or 4 dashes of raspberry syrup, stir up with a spoon, and serve.

This is a delicate-tasting mixture, but a perusal of the ingredients will readily show that it is rather powerful and should not be indulged in excessively.

BRANDY EGG NOG.

Use a mixing glass.

1 teaspoonful of sugar.
1 fresh egg.
1-3 glass of ice.
1 wine glass of brandy (Martel).

1 pony glass of Jamaica rum.

Fill the glass with milk.

Shake well in a shaker, strain into large bar glass, grate a little nutmeg on top, and serve with straws.

This is a very swell drink, and, like all other drinks where an egg forms a component part, is very nutritious.

SHERRY COBBLER.

Use a mixing glass.

$\frac{1}{2}$ teaspoonful of sugar.

1 wine glass of seltzer to dissolve sugar.

1 slice of pineapple.

1 slice of orange.

Fill the glass with fine ice, then fill with sherry wine; mix well, decorate with pineapple, orange and berries in season, and serve with straws.

Extremely popular in the family circle, as it can be absorbed by ladies and moderate drinkers without any injurious effects.

POUSSE CAFE.

Use a pousse cafe glass.

1-6 glass of raspberry syrup.

1-6 glass of maraschino.

1-6 glass of green vanilla.

1-6 glass of curacoa (red).

1-6 glass of chartreuse (yellow).

1-6 glass of brandy (Hennessey).

In mixing this drink great care should be exercised to have the lines separating the various ingredients clear and distinct, and if this is done you will have the prettiest-appearing drink imaginable.

SURE CURE.

Use a small bar glass.

½ spoonful of sugar.

10 drops of Dr. Tucker's No. 59.

2 dashes of peppermint.

½ pony glass of brandy (Hennessey).

½ pony glass of Sloe gin.

½ pony glass of cherry rum.

Stir well with spoon, grate a little nutmeg on top, and serve.

For persons afflicted with diarrhœa or dysentery the above mixture is almost infallible.

CHAMPAGNE SOUR.

Use a champagne goblet.

1 lump of loaf sugar.

1 dash of lime juice.

93

1 slice of orange.

1 slice of pineapple.

A few blackberries, if in season.

Fill up the glass slowly with champagne, spoon well, and serve.

This is a tart, palatable mixture, indulged in very extensively by the sporting fraternity.

WHISKEY RICKEY.

Use a medium size bar glass.

1 or 2 lumps of ice.

Squeeze the juice of one lime.

1 wine glass of whiskey.

Fill the glass with plain soda or vichy, and serve with a spoon.

Preferred by persons who are impartial to the flavor of gin, and considered by many superior in flavor to the gin rickey.

GOLDEN FIZZ.

Use a mixing glass.

1 spoonful of sugar.

2 or 3 dashes of lemon juice.

1 wine glass of Tom gin.

1 egg (the yolk only).

94

Fill the glass with fine ice.

Shake well with a shaker, strain into a fizz glass, fill up the glass with vichy or seltzer, mix well with a spoon, and serve.

MORNING REVIVER.

Use a mixing glass.

1 spoonful of sugar.
3 dashes of lemon juice.
1 dash of bitters (Angostura).
3 dashes of absinthe.
1 wine glass of whiskey.

Shake well with a shaker, strain into a fizz glass, fill up with seltzer, and serve.

When a person awakes in the morning with a desire for a stimulant and does not know what it shall be, the reviver will invariably fill the bill.

STIFFERINE.

Take a punch glass, put in ¾ of a glass of Bacon bitters, add a little grenadine mixed with soda, and serve.

95

PUNCH VICTOR HUGO.
(For a Party.)

2 bottles of claret.

1 bottle of Rhine wine.

1 pint of Imperial Sec.

½ pint of curacoa.

1 pound of sugar.

1 lemon, sliced.

1 orange, sliced.

Strawberries, if in season.

Put in pot to boil; when cool, put in a little Jamaica rum; keep in a punch bowl, and serve in small glasses.

POUSSE L'AMOUR.

Use a sherry wine glass.

¼ glass of maraschino.

The yolk of one fresh egg.

¼ glass of chartreuse (green).

¼ glass of brandy (Hennessey).

Attention should be paid to have the egg fresh and cold, and in mixing use a graduating glass.

This has the highest consideration among ladies in the theatrical profession and those who have been abroad, and is of French origin.

96

CREME DE MENTHE "COLUMBIA."

Use a cocktail glass.

Fill with shaved ice.

White creme de menthe, little sprig of mint on the side of the glass, small quantity of parfait d'amour; serve with straws. Be careful not to serve too cold.

CHAMPAGNE CUP.

(For Party of Six).

Use glass pitcher.

2 wine glasses of seltzer.

6 lumps of sugar dissolved in seltzer.

1 pony glass of benedictine.

1 pony glass of maraschino.

1 wine glass of brandy (Martel).

3 slices of pineapple.

3 slices of orange.

1 piece of ice.

Take one quart of champagne, pour on top, serve in champagne glasses.

For persons accustomed to the good things of life, champagne cup is considered the par excellence of all mixtures, and it must be conceded their verdict cannot be contradicted.

97

BROMO SELTZER.

Use two fizz glasses.

1 wine glass of water in each glass.

2 spoonfuls of bromo seltzer.

Mix from one glass to the other, and drink while foaming.

This is one of the best known and most speedy cures for a headache known to the professsion, and is perfectly harmless in its results.

EGG MILK PUNCH.

Use a mixing glass.

1 teaspoonful of sugar.

1 wine glass of brandy (Hennessey).

1-3 wine glass of St. Croix rum.

1 fresh egg.

Fill the glass with milk and put in fine ice.

Shake well, strain into a large bar glass, grate a little nutmeg on top, and serve with straws.

LADIES' DELIGHT.

Use a pony glass.

Three-fourths of a glass of apricot brandy, and fill the glass with cream.

This mixture is as smooth and delicate to the taste as the richest confections.

98

BRANDY MILK PUNCH.

Use a mixing glass.

1 spoonful of sugar.

1 wine glass of brandy (Martel).

½ pony glass of St. Croix rum.

Half fill the glass with fine ice, fill up with milk, shake well, strain into a large bar glass, grate a little nutmeg on top, and serve with straws.

This punch is unsurpassed in flavor if the best of liquors and rich milk are used, and should be served very cold.

IRISH WHISKEY COCKTAIL.

Use a mixing glass.

Half fill with fine ice.

1 dash of gum syrup.

2 or 3 dashes of orange bitters.

1 or 2 dashes of benedictine.

2-3 wine glass of Irish whiskey.

Mix well with a spoon, strain into a cocktail glass, and serve with an olive.

ROYAL HIGH BALL.

Use a high ball glass.

2 small lumps of ice.

1 wine glass of Royal Scotch whiskey.

Twist the rind of a lemon and fill the glass with seltzer, and serve with a spoon. Use nothing but Royal Scotch whiskey in mixing this drink.

YALE PUNCH.

Use a punch glass.

1 teaspoonful of sugar dissolved in a little water.

2 or 3 dashes of lemon juice.

1 or 2 dashes of lime juice.

2 or 3 dashes of raspberry syrup.

2 or 3 dashes of benedictine.

½ pony glass of St. Croix rum.

1 wine glass of brandy (Hennessey).

Fill the glass with fine ice, mix well with a spoon, decorate the top with two or three sprigs of mint, also with fruit in season, and serve with straws.

This punch derives its name from the fact of its popularity with students, not only at Yale, but other colleges where they desire everything of the best.

MINT JULEP.

Use a mixing glass.

1 small spoonful of sugar.

½ wine glass of seltzer.

4 or 5 sprigs of fresh mint; press them well in the sugar and seltzer until the flavor of the mint is extracted.

1½ glasses of brandy (Hennessey).

Fill the glass with fine ice, shake well, then take some sprigs of mint and insert them in the ice so the leaves will be in the shape of a bouquet; decorate with fruit in season, dash with Jamaica rum, sprinkle a little pulverized sugar on top, and serve with straws.

A great favorite with slow drinkers who are fond of something which leaves an aromatic flavor in their mouths.

WHISKEY CRUSTA.

Take a small lemon and cut off the ends, peel off the whole rind and place it inside of a wine glass, rub a slice of lemon around the edge of the glass, dip the glass in pulverized sugar. Mix as follows, using a mixing glass:

2 dashes of gum syrup.

1 dash of bitters (Angostura).

1 dash of lime juice.

2 dashes of benedictine.

1 wine glass of whiskey.

Half fill glass with fine ice, mix well and strain into a wine glass, dress with berries, and serve.

A combination which does not have to take a back seat for delicacy of flavor, and is becoming more in demand from day to day.

DROPPED ABSINTHE.

Use a mixing glass.

Half fill with fine ice.

3 dashes of anisette.

1 pony of absinthe.

Place the pony glass in the ice, take a small pitcher of ice water and drop the water slowly into the absinthe contained in the pony glass; remove the glass, and serve.

ABSINTHE FRAPPÉ.

Use a mixing glass.

Pack the glass full of fine ice.

2 or 3 dashes of anisette.

½ wine glass of absinthe.

Shake until the outside of the shaker is white with frost, strain into a star champagne glass, fill up with seltzer, and serve.

COFFEE COCKTAIL.

Use a mixing glass.

1 spoonful of pulverized sugar.
1 fresh egg.
1 pony of brandy (Hennessey).
1 wine glass of port wine.

Half fill the glass with fine ice, shake well, strain into a fancy stem glass, grate a little nutmeg on top, and serve.

The name of this drink is somewhat misleading, and is derived from the fact that if the drink is properly prepared it resembles coffee.

SAUTERNE COBBLER.

Use a mixing glass.

½ spoonful of sugar dissolved in a little seltzer.
1 or 2 slices of pineapple.
1 or 2 slices of orange.

Fill the glass with fine ice and the balance with sauterne, spoon well, decorate with fruit in season, and serve with straws.

A winner in extreme warm weather, as the percentage of alcohol is so small that it will not agitate the heart's actions and stimulate the circulation of the blood.

103

CHAMPAGNE PUNCH.

A la "Joanne d'Arc."

2 quarts of champagne (Champeret).
1 quart of sparkling Burgundy.
½ pound of sugar.
2 lemons, sliced.
2 oranges, sliced.
1 banana, sliced.
1 cucumber, sliced.

Mix together in a small punch bowl, and serve in small punch glasses. Fruit of all kinds, in their season, should be used in the punch and served with the same.

This concoction, like all others in which champagne forms the principal part, can not be otherwise than a palate tickler.

CLARET CUP.

(For a Party of Eight.)

Use a glass pitcher.

1 pint of Apollinaris.
6 large spoonfuls of powdered sugar; dissolve well.
5 or 6 sprigs of mint, well masticated.
1 pony of benedictine.
1 pony of curacoa (orange).

104

1 pony of maraschino.

1 wine glass of brandy (Hennessey).

4 slices of orange.

1 cucumber, sliced; save the skin to dress the pitcher.

4 slices of pineapple.

Berries, in season.

1 clean piece of ice.

Pour one quart of claret on top and dress the pitcher with a few sprigs of mint, stems down; dash the bouquet with Jamaica rum and sprinkle with powdered sugar, and serve in star champagne glasses. In slicing the cucumber place the skin in the pitcher so a small portion will hang over the top and the ends extend into the glass, placing one on each side of the pitcher, and with the mint in the centre makes a very attractive bouquet.

GIBSON GIRL.

Use a pousse cafe glass.

1-5 glass of creme de anisette.

1-5 glass of parfait d'amour.

1-5 glass of creme yvette.

1-5 glass of chartreuse (yellow).

Top off with whipped cream.

105

As modern and attractive as the Gibson pictures and as palatable as it is handsome, and for a smooth concoction is the accepted friend of the many resorts, both inland and on the coast; and no matter where the élite may be, they will call for their prime favorite, the Gibson Girl.

RHINE WINE CUP.

(For a Party of Six.)

Use a glass pitcher.

1 split of Apollinaris water.
4 spoonfuls of sugar; dissolve well.
5 or 6 sprigs of mint, well masticated.
1 pony of maraschino.
1 pony of white curacoa.
1 wine glass of very pale brandy.
4 slices of orange.
4 slices of pineapple.
Berries, in season.
1 clean piece of ice.
Pour one quart of Rhine wine on top, and dress the pitcher with cucumber rinds, and serve in star champagne glasses.

A drink mostly called for by the Germans and by them considered superior to the more expensive champagne cup.

MUSTY ALE.

Use large glass or pewter mug.

Two-thirds fill with old ale.
One-third fill with lager beer.

COFFEE KIRSCH.

Use a mixing glass.

Half fill with fine ice.
1 wine glass of kirschwasser.
1 pony of brandy.
2 dashes of maraschino.
1 small cup of black coffee.
Shake well, strain into a fancy stem glass, and serve.

HOT RUM PUNCH.

Use a hot water glass.

1 or 2 lumps of sugar dissolved in one-half glass of water.
1 dash of lemon juice.
1 wine glass of Medford rum.
Spoon well, grate a little nutmeg on top, and serve.

A cold-weather reviver, to stimulate the heart's action and create a good circulation.

DALY'S SUNBURST.

1 pony of brandy.

Add ice-cold milk; spoon well, to prevent curdling; drop yolk of fresh cold egg in same, using care not to break yolk of egg, and serve.

SAUTERNE CUP.

(For a Party of Eight.)

Use a glass pitcher.

1 pint of Apollinaris.

6 large spoonfuls of sugar; dissolve well.

5 or 6 sprigs of mint, well masticated.

1 pony of benedictine.

1 pony of curacoa (white).

1 pony of maraschino.

1 wine glass of brandy (Hennessey).

4 slices of orange.

1 cucumber, sliced; save the skin to dress the pitcher.

4 slices of pineapple.

1 clean piece of ice.

Pour one quart of sauterne on top, and dress the pitcher with a few sprigs of mint, stems down; dash the bouquet with Jamaica rum and sprinkle with powdered sugar, and serve in star champagne glasses. In slicing the cucumber place the skin in the pitcher so a small portion will extend over the top and the ends extend into the glass, placing one piece on each side of the pitcher so a small portion will hang over the top and the ends extend into the glass, placing one end of the peel on each of the four sides of the pitcher, the ends down; and, with the sprigs of mint, makes an excellent bouquet.

HOT WHISKEY COCKTAIL.

Use hot whiskey glass.

1 lump of loaf sugar.

Half fill the glass with hot water.

1 dash of Angostura bitters.

Fill the glass with whiskey, twist a piece of lemon peel on top, and serve.

A warm friend with persons who are driving or automobiling in cold weather and have become chilled, as it quickly revives them and makes them feel in their normal condition.

RUM COOLER.

Use a mixing glass.

1 spoonful of pulverized sugar.

109

¼ glass of water to dissolve sugar.

3 or 4 dashes of lemon juice.

Fill up the glass with fine ice, the balance with rum; shake well in a shaker, and serve with straws.

AFTER-DINNER COMPANION.

Use small china cup.

Three-quarters fill with hot black coffee, add one lump of loaf sugar, put in one pony of brandy, ignite and serve in presence of customer.

DARK SECRET.

Use thin bar glass.

1 bottle of ice-cold sarsaparilla.

1 pony of gin.

3 dashes of checkerberry.

Spoon well, and serve.

Among the colored 400 this wins the cake against all competitors.

PAWNBROKER'S DELIGHT.

Use large thin goblet.

1 pony of Russian allash.

1 pony of maraschino.

1 lump of clear ice.

Fill the glass with club soda and add three thin slices of lime, and serve.

BANKER'S PUNCH.

Use a mixing glass.

3 dashes of raspberry syrup.

1 spoonful of powdered sugar dissolved in seltzer.

Juice of one whole lime.

1 wine glass of whiskey.

1 pony glass of Jamaica rum.

Fill the glass with shaved ice, and spoon well; take a large punch glass, put in four or five blackberries, four or five raspberries, one slice of pineapple; mash in bottom of glass, so as to extract juice; then pour the mixture into punch glass, on top of mashed fruit, and serve.

This is much sought after by bankers and brokers and considered by them unequalled.

AUTOMOBILE.

Use a large, thin goblet.

1 lump of loaf sugar.

2 dashes of aromatic bitters.

1 dash of white curacoa.

111

2 dashes of creme yvette.
2 thin slices of pineapple.
1 thin slice of orange.

Put in small lump of clear ice and fill glass with imported champagne.

This is the very latest concoction devised by the author, and he respectfully submits judgment to connoisseurs.

FROSTED COCKTAIL.

Use a mixing glass.

2 or 3 dashes of gum syrup.
2 or 3 dashes of orange bitters.
1 or 2 dashes of benedictine.
½ jigger of whiskey.
½ jigger of French vermuth.

Fill up the glass with fine ice; spoon well; then take a cocktail glass and rub a piece of lemon around the edge, dip the glass in pulverized sugar; strain the ingredients into the cocktail glass, put in olive, twist a piece of lemon peel on top, and serve.

MAMIE TAYLOR.

Use high ball glass.

Juice of half a lime.
1 or 2 small lumps of ice.

1 wine glass of Scotch whiskey.

Fill up the glass with ginger ale, and serve with a bar spoon.

The foregoing offers a pleasing form for persons to partake of whiskey without feeling the harsh effect that plain whiskey would have, and imparts the same stimulating effect.

SAM WARD.

Peel a bright, clean lemon in one long string; arrange same around inside of a fancy stem glass; fill centre with shaved ice, fill one-third full of kümmel, fill one-third full of yellow chartreuse; add Cognac to fill glass, and serve with small straws.

This delicious decoction was devised by the famous New York connoisseur, after whom it was named; and by gentlemen who are on affectionate terms with their palates and stomachs is as fondly considered as their wives and sweethearts.

MISS MAZIE.

Use a mixing glass.

1 wine glass of port wine.

1 fresh egg.

113

2 or 3 dashes of raspberry syrup.

Half fill with fine ice.

Fill with rich, fresh milk.

Shake well; pour into straight, thin bar glass; sprinkle a very small quantity of ground cinnamon on top, and serve.

This formula was prepared by a young lady resident of Rhode Island who was in poor health and who had been directed by her physicians at various times to partake of the several ingredients separately; but, as they did not seem to attain the desired effect, she concluded to indulge in all at the same time, the result of which was that she rapidly regained her strength and vigor and was enabled to dispense with the use of medicines and enjoy life as a healthy young person should. The lady in question, learning of the author's intention of publishing this work, very considerately furnished the foregoing formula as a boon to persons who are run down or debilitated; and feels assured, from her personal experience, it will rapidly rebuild a weakened constitution.

114

TIM AND JACK.

Use large china mug.

1 spoonful of Baker's cocoa.

1 spoonful of sugar; dissolve in a little hot water.

½ jigger of Cognac.

½ jigger of St. Croix rum.

Fill mug with hot milk; stir well, and serve with spoon.

This is the most recent cold-weather resuscitater, and as a nourishing stimulant is unsurpassed.

PING PONG COCKTAIL.

Use a mixing glass.

2 or 3 dashes of wormwood bitters.

1 dash of ginger cordial.

2-3 jigger of Tom gin.

1-3 jigger of Scotch whiskey.

Fill up the glass with fine shaved ice; mix well with a spoon, strain into a cocktail glass, put in a cherry, twist a piece of orange peel on top, and serve.

115

ANGOSTURA AND SHERRY.

2 dashes of Dr. Siegert's Angostura bitters.

Fill glass with good sherry wine.

The above makes a delightful and exhilarating appetizer; and, unlike the various cocktails, none of the ingredients are harmful.

Classic Cocktail Resource Guide

Some ingredients found in vintage cocktail guides are unavailable or hard to come by today. However, the creation of historically accurate cocktails is a growing hobby and with a bit of Internet research, you will find recipes for bitters and syrups online, as well as manufacturers that are developing new product lines for the classic cocktail enthusiast.

Vendors
A short selection of online vendors selling bitters, mixers, syrups, wine, liqueurs, and spirits. This list is by no means complete but is a good place to start your search.

BevMo!
www.bevmo.com

Binny's Beverage Depot
www.binnys.com

The Bitter Truth
www.the-bitter-truth.com

Cocktail Kingdom
www.cocktailkingdom.com

Fee Brothers
www.feebrothers.com

Hi-Time Wine Cellars
www.hitimewine.net

Internet Wines and Spirits
www.internetwines.com

The Jug Shop
www.thejugshop.com

Monin Gourmet Flavorings
www.moninstore.com

Trader Tiki's Hand-Crafted Exotic Syrups
www.tradertiki.com

The Whiskey Exchange
www.thewhiskyexchange.com

General Interest
These sites provide background information on individual ingredients, suggestions for substitutes, current commercial availability, and recipes.

The Chanticleer Society
A Worldwide Organization of Cocktail Enthusiasts
www.chanticleersociety.org

Drink Boy
Adventures in Cocktails
www.drinkboy.com

The Internet Cocktail Database Ingredients Search
www.cocktaildb.com/ingr_search

Museum of the American Cocktail
www.museumoftheamericancocktail.org

WebTender Wiki
www.wiki.webtender.com

Coming Soon from
Classic Cocktail Guides
and Retro Bartender Books

Cooling Cups
and Dainty Drinks

A Collection of 19th-Century Cocktails Perfect
for Civil War Reenactments
and Victorian Theme Parties

William Terrington

Illustrations from
"American Dancing Master and Ball-Room Prompter"
by Elias Howe

Now Available from Classic Cocktail Guides
and Retro Bartender Books

Jack's Manual of Recipes for Fancy Mixed Drinks and How to Serve Them

A Pre-Prohibition Cocktail Book

J. A. Grohusko

ISBN: 978-1-880954-28-7

Now Available from Classic Cocktail Guides
and Retro Bartender Books

The Twentieth-Century Guide for Mixing Fancy Drinks

A Pre-Prohibition Cocktail Book

James C. Maloney

ISBN: 978-1-880954-29-4

Now Available from Classic Cocktail Guides
and Retro Bartender Books

The Ideal Bartender

Cocktails and Mixed Drinks
from the Years of the First World War

Tom Bullock
Bartender of the Pendennis Club, Louisville, Kentucky
and of the St. Louis Country Club

Introduction by George H. Walker
Grandfather to President George Herbert Walker Bush
and Great-Grandfather to President George Walker Bush

ISBN: 978-1-880954-31-7

Now Available from Classic Cocktail Guides
and Retro Bartender Books

Nineteenth~Century
Cocktail Creations

How to Mix Drinks: A Bar Keeper's Handbook

George Winter

ISBN: 978-1-880954-30-0

Now Available from Classic Cocktail Guides
and Retro Bartender Books

The Complete Bartender

The Art of Mixing Cocktails, Punches,
Egg Noggs, Smashes, Sangarees, Slings,
Cobblers, The Fizz, Juleps, Flips, Toddys,
Crustas, and All Plain and Fancy Drinks
in the Most Approved Style

Albert Barnes

ISBN: 978-1-880954-33-1

Now Available from
Historic Cookbooks of the World

Recipes of the Highlands and Islands of Scotland

A Classic Scottish Cookbook

Compiled by
An Comunn Gaidhealach

Originally published as
"The Feill Cookery Book"

ISBN: 978-1-880954-25-6

Now Available from
Historic Cookbooks of the World

Recipes of Sweden

A Classic Swedish Cookbook

Compiled by
Inga Norberg

ISBN: 978-1-880954-27-0